PURPOSE VISION *life*

A Collective Perspective from Five Visionary Authors

BY DEBRA WRIGHT OWENS

Published and distributed in the United States by Encore Empowerment International, LLC

All scripture references and quotations, as marked KJV, are taken from the King James Version of the Bible (public domain).

Written by Debra Wright Owens, Sarah Reid, Adrienne Gray, Beverly Vann-Woods, and Sharon K. Gipson

Book Cover design by Jasmin Mann
MannJasmin@yahoo.com

Paperback ISBN – 978-0-578-66565-8
Printed in the United States of America

Dedication

This book is dedicated to the *"Life, Vision and Purpose"* of ALL individuals aspiring to live their best life making positive contributions to the world. I call you Visionaires! May you be informed, inspired and empowered to passionately live your life with vision and purpose.

ACKNOWLEDGEMENTS

All praises and honor to God, the most high, for extending an impartation of *"Life, Vision and Purpose"* to me. I am grateful and don't take it likely, that I've been given an assignment to inform, inspire and empower others to passionately pursue their God-given purpose and vision.

I am thankful to my family and friends for their ongoing support of all my purposeful and visionary endeavors. I thank my children (Jasmin and Marius) who continuously inspire me to do more, and always bring me joy. I thank my spiritual leaders (Pastors Donald and Sarah Johnson) who continuously teach me faith in all things.

I extend honorable and special thanks to the contributing authors in this book: **Sarah Reid, Adrienne Gray, Beverly Vann-Woods and Sharon Gipson**; for sharing your up-close and personal perspectives on life, vision and purpose! I am grateful to each of you for sharing a part of yourself on this public platform. Your stories on life, vision and purpose have blessed me immensely.

I am grateful for my team members who helped me put this book together and make it available to you.

CONTENTS

PART FOUR
BEVERLY VANN-WOODS

PART FIVE
SHARON GIPSON

life VISION PURPOSE

INTRODUCTION

What is the meaning of life? Although many offer different definitions, perspectives and views on the meaning thereof, I believe that aside from life referring to a living-breathing organism, life does indeed have different meanings. They say that life is for living; but how many people do we know truly "live"? I have to ponder on this question myself! One thing that I can personally attest to; is that life is a journey - with many encounters along the way! Sometimes we are on the mountain top and at other times we are down in the valley low. Yet still we rise to the occasion of life! So, how do you navigate through life productively? What do you think your life's purpose is? Where do you see yourself going in life? What do you see yourself doing in life? Who do you see yourself becoming? Some of you may already have the answers to these questions figured out, and others of us are still on a quest for answers to these questions!

Life is full of experiences, both good and not so good. And as we have heard and continue to hear, we get out of life what we put in life. In other words, our choices and experiences shape our life, whether we realize it or not.

In this biographical collective, five visionary authors share their up close and personal perspectives on life, vision and purpose, through the lens of their very own "real-time" life experiences. Sometimes sharing your story is a movement in and of itself, and also the very step of faith that is needed to propel you into greatness, allow you to exhale, and *UNMUTE YOUR MESSAGE* to the world. In a compelling move of transparency, each author gives you a glimpse of their life, vision and purpose, through the lens of authenticity. Through the pages of this book, you get to experience a layer of each author, and journey with them through some of their most life changing and defining experiences.

Your life, your vision, your purpose; the common denominator here is you! Do you know your purpose? What is the *"thing"* that drives you? What are your life goals and desires? What obstacles and roadblocks are stopping you from living your best life? Are you living the fulfilled life that you desire? Or, are you at a crossroad –

not knowing which direction to choose? Are you sitting on the sidelines, waiting to get in the game of life? Well guess what, you're up next – it's your turn. That's right! It's your turn and time, to live the fulfilled life that you have longed to live. It is time for you to maximize your potential and impact the world. It is time for you to live healthier, wealthier, and fulfilled. It's time for you to step into your purpose. It is time to take action. It's time for you to break out and break free; RECLAIM YOUR LIFE! You do not have you walk in the shadow of others. Make a commitment <u>today</u> to reverse the course of mediocre. Face your giants with confidence and don't back down. Your life, purpose and vision are depending on you to persevere. Don't give up or give. You've got exactly what it takes to rewrite your story and narrate it yourself. You are a natural born winner; doubt and fear is not your portion. You were created by the creator to be creative, and your uniqueness is your extraordinaire superpower. *It's time for you to move beyond just existing to living, excelling and thriving!* You were born to shine and blaze trails. It's time for you to live your life and vision, on purpose.

PART ONE

DR. DEBRA WRIGHT OWENS

Life, Vision, Purpose AUTHOR SPOTLIGHT

Dr. Debra Wright Owens

Founder of Encore Empowerment International, LLC

Dr. Debra Wright Owens, a native Mississippian, is an EMPOWERMENT advocate, professional coach, speaker and minister; whose God-given purpose is to inform, inspire and Empower individuals to passionately pursue their vision and purpose. She is a practicing HR/LR professional with 33 years of federal service; having earned a PhD in Business Management, an MPA and BAS. She is a light and positive energy - full of vision, dreams and purpose. Dr. Debra has two amazing children, whom she truly adores.

Humble Beginnings

I'm not exactly sure if I would be totally correct to say that one never knows the hand that life will deal them. Sometimes we indeed know the outcome of situation, merely based on our choice in the matter. But, that is neither here nor there for what I'm sharing in this collective work, or least starting out. So, without further delay, I'll move right along!

While growing up as a child in the south, no one could have ever convinced me that by the age of thirty-five, I would be a twice divorced single parent with two children. That just would not have settled right with my "spirit". Not because I was evangelizing in my youth, but more so because I did not see myself fitting that pattern. Nevertheless, this truth became my reality. I have always considered myself to be a good person and make a sincere effort to treat people the way I want to be treated. I also make it a point to mind my own business. So how in the world did I end up twice divorced? I don't have all the answers to this question, but what I can tell you is that being a "good" person does not keep you married!

When I think back over the years, I realize that my life is a direct reflection of the choices I've made in the past and the choices I continue to make. Some of those choices were wise and some were not so wise. Some of those choices were truly based on a lack of knowledge, and some were made with me having full knowledge and foresight of the consequences.

I'm a country girl, born and raised in the deepest depths of the south. I grew up in the small rural town of Ruleville, Mississippi. My home town is full of southern hospitality and history. Civil Rights Activist Fannie Lou Hamer settled down in my small town, and her memorial resides there today. The population in Ruleville was slim to none; estimated at 2619 in 2019. When I left home in 1986, we had two family pharmacies, a Piggly Wiggly grocery store, a couple of quasi grocery stores owned by Asians, two banks, a couple of "dollar" stores and a couple of gas stations. Three sewing factories provided the towns people with jobs. My mother worked at two of those factories over the course of her life, before she became ill and had to retire. In the summer time, we even chopped cotton to make ends meet. Everyone knew each other in my hometown and it seemed everyone was related in some way. As a child, it was embedded in my head by my grandfather and mother, to get a good education, maintain my reputation, maintain my credit and don't let the little boys fool me into getting "knocked up". So, those are the areas I meditated and focused on while growing up.

I lived a very sheltered life growing up. I think because I am my mother's first born child, I was supposed to be a pattern or example for my siblings that followed after me. I was very responsible at a young age. I can remember cleaning my sister Tonya's soiled diapers in the toilet and taking care of her as if I was an adult. At the tender age of ten, I was cleaning an entire house and cooking a full dinner. During summer breaks from school, I would look after my sister Tonya, because we didn't have the extra money to pay an outsider to look after us. My mom truly taught me the ins and outs of taking care of a home – those duties and responsibilities that society say should be taken care of by females.

Memories of My First Loves

My mother, Mary Ann Wright, was a strong-beautiful black woman, and she worked her fingers to the bone to make a way for me and my two sisters. Although she was married to my step dad, she was the main provider for our family. She made more money, and always seemed to be the one who took care of things around the house. She taught me and my sisters life skills that carry us until this day! She taught us how to cook, clean, and be highly respectful humans – with morals and values. I can say with certainty that my mom was the glue that held our family down and together.

As a child, I spent a great deal of time with my grandfather, the late great Wilson Wright. He was the strong male-father figure in my life. He stood about 6 feet, 4 inches tall, and had a most honorable reputation that preceded him. He was well respected in our small town. I truly believed that my grandfather could literally do anything. Although he did not know how to read or write, he built houses, operated an upholstery business, raised a farm every year until his health no longer allowed, and hunted and processed meats. I remember once standing in my grandfather's kitchen, grinding deer meat into sausage, and adding sage, salt and pepper to season it just right. That ground deer meat with fat back taste like Jimmy Dean breakfast sausage, or better! I remember going to my grandfather's garden to pick fresh tomatoes, field peas and watermelon in season. We literally lived off of organic foods back in the day; from the garden to the meats!

I was sort of the first grandchild, if "sort of" makes sense. Let me explain. My grandfather had nine children (seven girls and two boys) with my biological grandmother, who he was married to. He also had two older sons before he met and married and my grandmother. I am the first grandchild from my mother's biological siblings. Although my older uncles have children older than I am, they were not in the picture at the time. We also learned many years later, that my grandfather had actually fathered a set of twins that no one knew about but him and the twins' mother; that's a story for a later time. My grandfather single-handedly raised my mother and her 8 siblings after my grandmother died a couple of weeks after my youngest aunt Sandra was born. They told me the story of how different people offered to take some of my aunts in and raise them after my grandmother passed away; but my grandfather refused to separate his children. Now that's a strong black man and father! Today, women can barely raise one child without stressing out! Time surely brings about a change. It just seems that our ancestors of old were built tough like Duracell batteries. When my grandfather's health began to decline back in the mid-80s, it hurt me to my core. His health failed him totally in 1991, as he passed away in the hospital. I will always remember how strong, smart and respected he was.

Although we didn't have much to do in my small hometown, I was really happy growing up. I remember laughing with my childhood friends until my side hurt. I remember playing kickball and dodge ball in the streets. I remember going to the neighborhood swimming pool during summer breaks from school. I remember sitting on the porch with my mom and sister, watching people and cars go by. I remember watching television until 12pm midnight, when the stations went off. Those were the good ole days; full of fun and memories.

On My Own – The Journey Begins

I graduated from Ruleville Central High School on May 30, 1986. By June 4, 1986, I was a soldier in the United States Army, attending basic training at Fort Jackson, South Carolina – Tank Hill. What a 180 degree turn! My Army days were days of growing and exploring life. They were days of becoming independent and making choices on my own. I was so "green" when I joined the Army, I didn't know what jailbait meant, as some of the older male soldiers shouted that word when I arrived at Nelligen Barracks in Stuttgart, Germany. I had no clue, but later learned that I was a target for thirsty wolves.

My first assignment to Germany was an interesting one. I was totally shocked when I learned that our living quarters were co-ed. That's right, males and females lived together in the barracks – as far back as 1986. Some of them "literally" lived together, if you get my drift. My first roommate was of Irish decent. Her name was Irene. She had an accent, red hair and big pretty eyes. She was really nice. I remember us going on sort of a double date once. We were exercising the Army's buddy system concept. We were told to never go anywhere without your buddy. So, that's what we practiced for a while, even when we were doing things that we should not have been doing. I don't remember how or when Irene and I split up, but my new roommate was Jocelyn from Queens, New York. When I tell you that Ms. Jocelyn was a tough cookie, believe me she was indeed! She had streets smart; something I had no clue of. But, Jocelyn watched out for me. It was as if she was assigned to be my big sister away from home. She would crack jokes about things passing over my head because I was from the south, but I learned a lot from just watching her. I actually learned to take a stand and speak up, just from watching Jocelyn in action while we were roommates.

I Said Yes!!!

I left Germany around October 1988 and reported to Ft. Sam Houston in San Antonio, Texas. By September 1989, I was a wife. Who would have thought I would be married so soon; especially when I really wasn't interested in getting married at the time. Nevertheless, I had said yes to a proposal because I did not have the sense or guts to say no. I actually said yes, because I felt "his" feelings would be hurt if I said no. That's a separate book too; if you get my drift. Here I was on my first marriage at the age of 21, with no clue of what I was doing. But I did the best I could. We were two different people trying to make a marriage work, when we didn't even know what marriage meant. On top of that, neither of us had a godly example to follow or no one close by to help guide us in the process. Although we both grew up in two-parent households, we didn't have "model" marriages to mimic.

I excelled in the military, as I've done throughout life; even with my valley experiences. Within my first year in the military, I had already attended my first leadership development course in Vilseck, Germany, and gone before the board to become a non-commissioned officer. I had so many experiences in the military. It would take me a great deal of time to go into all of them. I can truly say that by the grace of God, I was shielded and protected through my days of trying to find myself as a soldier in the United States Army. I left the Army in 1992, after the Desert Storm War Campaign began.

Happy Times in Chaos

There were lots of disagreements, many sleepless nights, and a great deal of chaos during my first marriage. I totally couldn't understand why he didn't get where I was coming from and vice versa. We were two different people, trying to make something work that truthfully wasn't meant to be. The truth hurts, but it will definitely set you free! I was trying to be a wife based on how I was raised, and he was trying to be a husband based on his up-bringing. He was a heavy drinker at the time, party goer and a "Rico Suave". I was a homebody. So we clashed – because he wanted to party all of the time, and I wanted to stay home and watch TV. In 1993 my beautiful daughter, Jasmin Camille Mann was born. I can honestly say that Jasmin was my first love (aside from my mom). Here she was - high yellow and just down right juicy and sweet. I kissed on that child so much when she was a baby. I was just in love with her. I thought how in the world could any human be so beautiful and precious. We held on for as long as we could, for ten years actually; until I made the decision to file for a divorce. It wasn't an easy decision; but I felt strongly that it was one I had to make.

Three years after my first divorce, I was trying my hand at marriage again. I actually thought my second marriage would stand the tests and trials, because I had rededicated my life to Christ, had gained "some" knowledge of God's word and was really excited about growing more in Christ and being married. Regardless of the RED flags waving way before I said "I DO" a second time, I said "YES" again! In 2000, my son (Prince Marius) was born, and once again I was in love. God had given me a male child to raise. Marius has always been a special child, and it seems I had more time raising him, since my life had started to slow down. On the other hand, things were rocky from the start of my second marriage, and needless to say - I was heading back to divorce court within two and a half years. This second divorce really hit home. It made me truthfully assess myself, and I reached the conclusion that I had said "yes" to two marriage proposals that I should not have! I won't "male bash" my ex-husbands, because neither of them are bad people – they were just the wrong people for me. I'm cordial with both of my exes until this day, as I've never been able to hold grudges and un-forgiveness in my heart. I see no value in doing so. Further, I clearly understand that life is all about choices; sometimes we choose wrong and sometimes we choose right! I've been divorced since 2004, and since that time I've gotten to know myself rather well. I've spent the past 15 years focusing on raising my children, who are now 26 and 19. I've also developed a very close relationship with God, advanced my education with completing my PhD, as well as developed personally and professionally. I have no idea of what tomorrow holds for me, in the arena of dating/marriage, but I'm open to unlimited possibilities (as long as God is at the center of it)!

Why Do We Settle?

Have you ever settled for mediocre or less than, when you knew you desired and deserved more? Truthfully, at some point and time, we all settle or have settled for mediocre or less than what we actually desire. Whether we settled for a job that we didn't want; a relationship that did not make us happy; a friendship that was draining; or way less money than we are worth – we have all settled at some point and time in our lives. Why do you think people settle for a moderate or not very good life, when deep down inside they desire more – and it is actually within their abilities and control to have and do more? Too often, many individuals offer excuses of why they can't live the life that they desire, but seldom do they take individual responsibility for settling for mediocre. Many set the blame on being dealt a bad hand in life. The blame generally is set on their upbringing, their environment, lack of money, or education - and the list goes on. Some even think that the life they truly desire is unobtainable for them. They see others living their dream life, but they lack the level of confidence necessary to pursue that lifestyle for themselves. Then there are those who waste a lot of time – watching television, scrolling social media, playing video games, and meddling in other people's matters. So they are not really focused on the things that would yield the rewarding life they desire. There are even those who do not want to put in the work to get the life they desire, or they give up as soon as things get tough, and then they complain that they never got what they wanted – so they live life dreaming and <u>wishing upon a star</u>. The good news is that life offers us all unlimited possibilities, and we can all have what you truly desire! So here's why you can't afford settle for mediocre:

- Right now, you are living the only life that you will ever have here on earth.
- You were created by the Creator to be creative.
- You were born with an assigned Purpose.
- The world is awaiting your genius and contribution.
- You are so extraordinary and unique, that you cannot be duplicated.
- Your mind has the capacity to THINK, DREAM, ENVISION, and CREATE the extraordinary life that you desire and deserve!

What do you truly desire in life? Whatever it is, however impossible it seems, never surrender, never give up on it, and never settle for anything less than that. Go for it, or die trying. That is the attitude of winners!

Building Blocks

Miriam Webster defines a building block as "a unit of construction or composition; or something essential on which a larger entity is based". We are all under construction – a work in progress, and every daily encounter, each trial, or desert experience we encounter along this walk called life, is a building block that adds to the ultimate construction of who we are, who we will ultimately become and our destined purpose. With each experience or building block, we should see a clearer picture of our construction – who we are becoming. Although we may become many titles and things throughout life, I believe that becoming is a continual process, until the very day we die.

Life Changing Events

There are times in our lives that we can't clearly see where we are going, but God already knows that we will get there. Even when we don't know the plans that God has for us or understand them, God knows and understands His plans for us. In Jeremiah 29:11, God declares, I know the plans I have for you; plans to prosper you and not to harm you, plans to give you hope and a future. I can remember back 22 years ago, when I was in a place that I could not understand (a place of despair, false hope, loneliness and confusion). But today, I know with certainty that God understood all alone. Now I can clearly understand that while I was going through the trials of two failed marriages, God was preparing me for a time such as this, a time when I would be in a position to inform, inspire and empower others; a time when I would share a summarized version of my story with others – in hopes to encourage them to believe that they don't have to settle and they can have more and greater. You see, I have been married and divorced twice. Yet today, I am still standing; strong as a willow tree with my feet planted and rooted deep in the word and will of God. I am a light, shining bright for all to see. In spite of my ups and down, I am still excited about life, vision and purpose. I clearly understand that life is what we make it. I understand that we have the power to frame our own world. Because I am human, I don't always live on the mountain's peak, but I know it's there. And even when I am not existing there physically, because of the cares of this world, my subconscious knows that I can be there, by faith and works.

The Meaning of Vision

What does vision mean? Google offers several definitions, such as "the faculty or state of being able to see; the ability to think about or plan the future with imagination or wisdom". From a biblical perspective, scripture at Habakkuk 2:2 says, "Then the Lord answered me and said, Write the vision And engrave it plainly on [clay] tablets, So that the one who reads it will run". Proverbs 29:18 states in part, "…Where there is no vision, the people perish". My personal thought, as a believer in Jesus Christ, is that vision is definitely important; because the bible speaks on vision. Further, we cannot get "there", if we don't have a vision or visual of where "there" is!

What is your vision? What do you see for yourself, on a short-term and long term basis? Vision is foresight, and gives you something to strive for. Vision is the small or big picture that you desire to obtain. Vision is the visual that you want to move towards and ultimately become. Vision is the fixed point that you desire to reach. Vision adds clarity to your navigation! Without vision, you're going in circles or you simply don't know where you are going. Vision is life!

Vision in Action

Write the vision and make it plain is what they say, right? So, let's assume that you have already done the first step and defined your vision. Where do you go from here? Well now you have to set it in stone. This simply means that you have to put the vision or visual that you have formed in your mind, into actual written words or on a vision board. Seeing your vision, your end goal, in the physical form of words or pictures is a continuous motivator and serves as a guide on your journey to fulfilling your vision. Doing so also allows you to memorialize your vision as a starting point for manifestation.

They always told me that actions speak louder than words. And I know from first- hand experience that this concept holds true! You can say what you are going to do all day long, but until you add "action" to the equation, you are just talking. So you may very well have put your vision into tangible form through words or pictures, but my question to you now is how will you get to the point of fulfilling your vision? How do you plan to navigate your vision to REALITY; to make it a living breathing manifestation of what you imagined forehand? To move beyond the visual to reality, you will need a plan. And who, what, where, when, and how...are all vision planning questions that you need to answer. Nothing can be built efficiently without some form of a plan, roadmap, strategy or blueprint. This applies to your vision, as well as any one's vision. Planning how you will move your vision "beyond the vision board" to reality, will ensure your vision successfully comes to life!

Fulfilling your vision is a "hands-on" activity. Physical ACTION is indeed a necessity. What good is a plan if no action is taken to fulfill it? How far you go on your journey to vision fulfillment all depends on your willingness to forward and take action on it. "How far can you go standing still?" Once you've developed a plan, you now have a guide to take action on your vision. Making your vision reality may be something as small as giving your business a name, setting aside money for that dream vacation, or registering for a course to continue your education. That small, yet mighty step will bring you even closer to bringing your vision forth. All it takes is a little action.

Once you have taken action on your visionary plans, and started to "work your vision", you should check your progress. Is your vision manifesting as you imagined? Is the reality of your vision meeting your expectations or does it need to be "tweaked" a bit? How far have you come on your journey to fulfilling your vision? How much progress have you made up until this point? Can you record measurable results yet? You may not be where you want to be just yet - but with defining your vision, putting it in tangible written or picture form, creating a plan for vision and implementing it; you should be better off than you were. Some progress is "definitely" better than none!

Trial and error are present in every aspect of life, to include bringing your life's vision into reality. If things aren't going quite as you have planned in life, it is perfectly okay and often necessary to make adjustments along the way. So, it is indeed common practice to adjust your vision periodically, as well as evolve your vision over time, to expand and achieve more or better results. It's actually a wise practice to adjust the vision for your life to achieve better results. As a matter of fact, the vision we have for our lives often change, as a result of our experiences along the way. Remember, everything changes! Publishing your first book is a great achievement, but don't stop there. Why not turn that one book into a series? Bring your vision to fruition and go beyond what you've imagined! Don't limit yourself.

Poised for Purpose

While driving home from a Sunday morning church service10 to 12 years ago, I stopped at a gas station to pick up a copy of a local newspaper. The newspaper featured a special section on then Democratic candidate for the 44th Presidency of the United States, Senator

Barack Hussein Obama. The special section contained several pictures of then Senator Obama at different phases of his life. Two of the pictures in particular captured my attention. One was a picture of Senator Obama as a child sitting on his mother's lap at play. The other was a young Obama on campus at Harvard in 1990, newly elected as head of the Harvard Law Review. I paused for a moment, then turned to my daughter Jasmin and asked, "I wonder did Obama ever say he wanted to be President of the United States while growing up?" Jasmin and I held a discussion about what we called, along with many other African Americans at the time, "history in the making". We even joked that we were going to make a scrap book memorializing newspaper articles on Obama during his presidential campaign. As a matter of fact, I told Jasmin that I was going to frame a picture of then Senator Obama, because I was proud and excited about "change"

That Sunday morning discussion with Jasmin led me into deep thought of who I had become up until that point in my life. As I continued driving home that Sunday morning, I asked myself, "Did I ever think I would be who I had become at that point?" The whole excitement about then Senator Obama's Presidential candidacy led me into a sense of realization and actualization. My mind began to revisit my life's past experiences, my present state, and my dreams and aspirations for the future. It was so overwhelming that I concluded that this was something I needed to capture in writing. So I began to write. Well that was 10 to 12 years ago, and as we all know, Senator Obama became the 44th President of the United States of America; and the first African American president in history – having served two consecutive terms in office!

I am not a politician hoping to one day become the President of the United States, and I am not a celebrity, except maybe on a small scale within my circle of influence. To sum it up, I am not world known – yet! I am a blood-bought believer in Jesus Christ, who knows with certainty that I have a purpose in life to become who God has predestined me to be.

It All Started to Make Sense

As I mentioned earlier in my writing, I was always told growing up, "get a good education- so you can get a good job". Well of course that was great advice. However, that same advice could have very well been the reason it took me years to move outside of myself and set out on a quest to understand the meaning of my existence; to seek out my purpose. Why was I born? Why am I here? What am I supposed to be doing? These are questions that started to plague my mind years ago; especially after my second divorce. You see, my mind had been conditioned from early on to work for others, which is definitely not all bad, but you have to know that there is more to life than getting up day-after-day for 30 to 40 years, to punch a clock and do work that does not soothe and satisfy your soul. I actually had that epiphany about 20 to 25 years ago. However, navigating my way to a point where I could take a leap of faith and launch out on my own did not come easy!

Bondage in Disguise

It is not always easy to break the bond with the hand that feeds you. Often times, we get comfortable on jobs, especially if it's a good paying job. If you have a good-steady paycheck coming in from the task master, why would you want to step out, and possibly struggle with starting your own business? Many would ask, "Why fix something that is not broken?" Truthfully, a job can be a friend or foe. If you have no desire to be an entrepreneur and own your own business, then landing a good job may be the perfect path for you. On the other hand, if you have an entrepreneurial spirit, with a great business idea, and desire to be your own boss, then a 9-5 job can become a foe to you- especially when you don't know when to let go or you're afraid to leave the comfortable lifestyle that your job provides. Don't get me wrong - jobs are not at all bad, but when you have a "nudging" in your spirit that just won't stop pulling at you, you have to stop and listen. In doing so, you will more than likely come to the realization that a 9 to 5 job is only a means to fund your true purpose and vision in life. So, don't ignore the "nudging" and overextend your stay. Know when to walk away!

Facing the Fear Giant

Fear is such a "dreaded" word: False Evidence Appearing Real. Fear has caused so many dreamers to settle and live their life "stuck" inside a box. Fear has caused so many individuals to abort their dream life, vision and purpose. Fear can stop us in our tracks and hold us captive for years, even a life-time, if we do not face it head on! Fear will tell you that you can't do it. Fear will tell you that you will fail. Fear will tell you that you don't have what it takes to pursue your heart's desires and go after you vision and dreams. The truth of the matter is that fear is a liar! We all have exactly what it takes to live the fulfilled life that we truly desire, on purpose. Once you believe and accept that you will not fail, you can live outside of the box!

If you only have faith the size of a mustard seed - you can speak to your mountain of fear, tell it to be cast aside - and move forward with pursuing your vision, purpose and dream life. Fear is just an illusion, and once it is faced head on and defeated, we realize that we were living in fear in vain. Don't let an illusion box you in and abort your dreams. Now that you have cast your fears aside, it's time to step out and reach for the stars.

A Changed Mindset

There comes a time in our life when change is necessary, especially if we desire more in life. We all have some things in our life that we desire to change, some dreams and desires that we want to pursue, but we somehow find ourselves waiting on the right time to make that change or pursue those dreams and desires. You may desire to start a business, but you're waiting until you get extra or enough money to do so. Maybe you desire to take a dream vacation, but you're waiting on the money to do so. You may even desire to lose weight, but are waiting on the right time to start that exercise program and eat healthy. Perhaps you've been putting off surrendering to God like you know that He wants you to, and you even desire to, but you're waiting for what you say is the right time to do so. So, what's keeping you from changing now - today?

Have you ever calculated the amount of time that has already passed since you have been waiting for the right time to make that change?

I remember working on a job some years back, where I worked nights, weekends, and holidays. I desired so much to change jobs because I literally hated working nights, weekends, and holidays. I recall saying that I would apply for another job when the time was right. Although I was making good money, I was not at all happy about my work schedule. Before I knew it, a decade had come and gone, and I was still there. One day, I finally decided to sit down at my computer and apply for jobs elsewhere, and guess what, I got another job. However, it took me eleven years to get up and do something different – to get up and do what was required to change the situation that I was in - that I did not like.

Often times, we are not making any progress; or the progress that we should be making in life, because we are just waiting and waiting! We say that we are waiting for the right time! When all we need to do is get up and by move by faith towards our change, desires, and dreams, and trust in God and His word that everything will work together for our good, according to God's will. How long have you been waiting and desiring change in your life? How long have been waiting to pursue your dreams and desires? How much longer are you willing to lie in the state you're in and continue waiting for the right time? How bad do you want change; how bad do you want more out of life?

Unfortunately, we immediately offer excuses as to why we are not living life to the fullest; being our best self in Christ - being who God says that we are. We blame our condition on others, or we live below our means or potentials on the thought that someone else is holding us back. Do you actually think that our Almighty Sovereign God would leave our destiny in the hands of another man? Who are you blaming today for you not living the life of victory and prosperity that God has promised you? In the bible story about the man waiting at the pool of Bethesda, Jesus did not give the man any handouts; neither did Jesus help the man get into the pool for the "troubling of the waters". Actually, what the man needed was not in the water!

Jesus simply told the man to "...GET UP, TAKE UP YOUR BED AND WALK"! Jesus spoke two words to the man - "GET UP!" And the man got up. You see, the man already had the potential to get up and change his situation, but he had become comfortable with where he was – whoa unto me and you, to ever think that we cannot do it! The man at the pool of Bethesda was waiting 38 long years for someone to come along and do for him, what he always had the potential to do for himself. "A changed mindset is a movement!"

Is your life right now reflecting what you really desire; or have you just become comfortable with where you are? Have you brought your expectations down to your state of being because you cannot see beyond where you are? If so, it is time for a change, and that change starts with changing your mindset!

Jesus already knew the man's potential, and spoke to that potential. I am speaking to you and your potential through the words on these pages. You have what it takes (the potential) to get up from any situation or circumstance that has fed you a lie about what you are capable of accomplishing in life. If you desire something different in life, then get up and change your life! Take up that very thing which has caused you to operate in a state of waiting; in a holding pattern, not making progress, not being productive, just existing, just surviving, having just enough, desiring more but not believing that you will have more. Use that thing to propel you to your next level of freedom and prosperity. Get up from where you are and go for it! The wait is over! Change is knocking at your door. You have what it takes to pursue and possess your desires and dreams. You have God and heaven backing you.

The time is NOW to get up! Get up and run after purpose, run after destiny, run after your desires, run after your dreams. Get up and take control of your life. Get up and run after vision, and don't look back. Get up and walk by faith. Get up and resuscitate those dry bones in your life – they shall live. Get up and resuscitate every promise that

God has made to you – they are not dead! Get up and stop complaining. Get up and work in the Kingdom. Get up and step out of yesterday into today! Get up and live your best life! Get up and press your way until you get a breakthrough. Get up out of your disappointments. Get up out of yesterday's failures. Get up out of last year's losses and into today's wins. Get up and speak to your mountains, and tell them to be removed and cast into the sea. Get up and tell the storms in your life to Peace BE STILL! Get up and speak to your infirmities and tell them to be thou healed in the name of Jesus. There is no reason for you to stay there where you are! There are no more excuses! You have to do something different to see change! You have to GET UP! Get up and move beyond just surviving or just getting by – to more than enough.

You have what it takes, get up and move by faith. If you don't get up, you will surely stay down! Jesus believes in you because he invested his very life in you. Believe in yourself. Get up and go for it. Get up and stay up!

PART TWO

SARAH REID

Life, Vision, Purpose AUTHOR SPOTLIGHT

Sarah Reid

Co-Founder of Georgia Girls Event Planners and R&R Stagers

Sarah loves her family, friends, and community. She is a certified paralegal, an avid reader and lifelong learner. She survived a traumatic brain injury (aneurysm) in 2016, which she talks more about in her upcoming book, "Sarah: An Aneurysm Survivor's Story". She is on her second life which includes her two businesses: R&R Stagers and Georgia Girls Event Planners. She is also the Secretary, and Board Member of the non-profit Visionaire Foundation, Inc. She is embracing her purpose in life.

Misinterpreted

I am the 3rd child in a family of six children. I was the middle child for the first 13 years of my life. Having two older siblings shielded me from having to speak for myself. So, in turn, it made me extremely shy. There are parts of my personality that still are.

Most recently, my Dad asked me, "What makes a person shy?" I was flooded with past memories. Being too shy to answer questions; not wanting to draw attention to myself; not asking for what I wanted; and not saying "no" to a lot of things. I thought about the question for several minutes before answering. I told him that there is a difference between interacting with others (shyness) and having an opinion. Most people thought because I did not talk a lot, that I did not have an opinion. I have always been a listener and an observer. When I am passionate about something, I voice my opinion. The delivery is not always the best, but they get the point. To deal with my shyness these days, I always have a buffer (friend) with me. A majority of my friends are talkers, so we tend to balance each other out in our vulnerable moments.

The First

I was the first in my family to attend and graduate from college. I enrolled as a Return-to-College student at Agnes Scott College in Decatur, Georgia, and graduated with the Class of 2001. College had its own challenges because I was an older student, and the student body was less than 22 years old. Our life experiences were different. I had been in the working world for at least 10 years. I knew what it was like to get up and go to work every day; to be in a job with no advancement opportunities. I wanted a career and the ability to grow personally and professionally. Agnes Scott helped me to broaden my perspective on life. At Agnes Scott, I began to see things differently; to understand things differently. While there, I worked 10-15 hours a week as a part of their media team. I did not realize it at the time, but Agnes Scott prepared me for my future in Staging and Event Planning.

The Itch

After graduation, I continued to work in banking for the next 5 years. It was during the recession of 2008 that I was given a reality check. One night, the Operations manager gathered all the employees for a meeting. He told us that we were lucky that our bank was bought out by Wells Fargo. He went on to say, had that not occurred, we would have arrived at work and the doors would have been locked; no notice given to us - nothing. I was devastated. I suspect that management was given prior notice, and had time to prepare for the inevitable. After that meeting, I started searching for other opportunities in the field that I had chosen, because at the time, I was working full-time at night and enrolled at a technical college working towards a Paralegal Degree. I was still aiming for that career that I wanted, and sometimes needed. After two internships, one in Fulton County Court System and the other in the law office of a reputable attorney, I was able to complete my degree in 2007. Believe it or not, it took me another two years to get into the legal field where I am currently working. But you know, I still have that itch; the itch that started many years ago - the desire to start my own business. Not having an idea of what my business venture would be. What were my skills? What was I good at? Was I talented? These thoughts plagued me. Yet, I would put them off for a few more years.

Still feeling that itch, I began to think about the things that I did for free. Things that brought me joy in doing them. I remember being at home and a classmate called me. She told me that they were having a fundraiser for a neighbor and asked me to come down (I live 73 miles away). She went on to say that they wanted to discuss the upcoming class reunion and wanted me to head it up. I asked her, "What is going on?" Unbeknownst to me, they had been discussing the reunion and me, prior to calling me. My classmate had attended the 15th class reunion picnic that I had put together. I think about 20 classmates actually came to the event. But it was the organization of it all that stayed with them. I created the menu, hired the cook, asked everyone to bring something, provided the music, and the decorations. It turned out to be a very memorable event. One in which, when they needed a planner for the 30th, I was the first person to come to mind.

I remember one of the conversations I had with my cousin around 2015. He was creating a photo disk for me. He told me that I was an event planner. He said, "Sarah you are always putting together events for other people. You are dedicated and organized. You think of all the little details; like creating a disk for all the classmates, past and present. I didn't give our conversation much thought, even though I was in the middle of planning our 30th class reunion.

I put on several more family reunions after that initial conversation with my cousin. He and I teamed up to create an event for the annual family Christmas party. It was one of the best holiday celebrations that I can recall. Fast forward to 2016.

And Then the Unexpected

I was getting ready for my "girls-trip" that was to take place on May 11, 2016. My friend was traveling from Jacksonville, Florida to Georgia. We had planned to take a road trip from Georgia to Birmingham to Memphis and back. The evening before, I went to the gym to get my last work-out in. I remember doing my back exercises. *Then, I got the worst headache that I have ever experienced.* I tried to sit down, but I couldn't. I laid down on the mat, while holding my head in my hands and screaming. I finally called 911. I could not remember the address to the building, nor the name of the church.

A security officer walked in and saw me. He asked me if I was okay. I told him that my head was hurting and that I had called 911. I did not know the address. I asked him to talk to the operator and give her the information. Another staff member came in, asking me questions. Who should she call? Who did she need to notify? I gave her my sister's name and number. The call went unanswered. I gave her my Dad's number. He answered on the 2nd ring. They told him that I had been in an accident and they were waiting on the ambulance to arrive. They said that someone would call him back later to let him know what was going on. My Dad was alarmed. He was working outside and decided to put up his tools. He went inside the house, took a bath, and waited. He called my sister several times. She had just started a part-time job, but finally answered when her shift was over. He told her that someone from the church had called. They told him that I had an accident, but no one had called back. My sister knew the gym I attended and the area of the nearest hospital. She made a few calls and found me. She then called Dad and gave him the address and location of the hospital I was in.

After the ambulance and paramedics arrived, I answered their questions. They loaded me onto the stretcher and placed me in the ambulance. I was unconscious before we reached the hospital. When I regained consciousness (woke up), my sister was in the bed with me. I asked her not to talk aloud because my head was pounding. If you know my sister, then you know she talks aloud and has a country twang. I lost consciousness again.

My memory began to come back when I was in my second week of rehabilitation. I was told that I had a brain aneurysm; that I had trauma to the left side of my brain - which is why I was paralyzed on the right side of my body. I spent 43 days total (2 weeks in intensive care, 1 week in a regular room, and the remainder in rehab) between the hospital and rehab. My time in rehab was intensive. I had cognitive and physical therapy. Every day I was taking some type of therapy. Everything was a test. Looking back on it, I believe they were assessing our memory; how much was retained - determining areas that we needed to work on. Remember earlier, when I told you that I was shy. Well imagine being in therapy and you cannot communicate that you are right handed. For at least two weeks they thought that I was left handed. *Hell, I thought I was left handed.* My memory started coming back and I had to find a way to communicate those things. I was eating or shall I say drinking everything with my left hand. Mostly, I just stared at my food. One of the attendants would sometimes help me by placing the silverware in my hand. Needless to say, I was starving by dinner time. But thankfully, my Dad stayed with me at rehab and was there to feed me. Yes, if you must know, I'm spoiled.

The entire time I entered the hospital I was never alone. My dad, mother, sister, brother, family, and friends were constant. Those first few weeks were crucial for me. I could not speak for myself. My sister became my advocate. I could not pray for myself. My community, classmates, churches, friends, family, and their friends prayed for me. I could not make decisions. My dad made the critical decisions that mattered.

The Journey Back to Me

I spent my 49th Birthday in Rehab. My friend Jan brought the music, party hats, and deserts. Carmen delivered the gifts and flowers from work. Tracy brought the food and balloons. My cousin Yolanda and friend Luz called to wish me a Happy Birthday. That was on the 8th, I was not scheduled to leave until the 22nd. But we partied as if it was my last day there. We danced and enjoyed ourselves. For a little while, I could imagine myself as being normal.

I had a few more weeks to take advantage of my therapy sessions. I worked daily to strengthen my mind and my body. As it got closer to my release date, my paralysis was releasing a hold on me. My leg was back to normal functioning. My hand would take a little longer. I was using the medicine ball several times a day. When I was released from the hospital, I was on a walker, for one week. Then I was using the walking cane to get around. I continued to use the medicine ball, until one day I realized that I no longer needed it. My hand had returned to normal functioning.

I continued to take therapy. For three weeks cognitive and physical therapists came to my home. The additional 5 weeks I was as an outpatient at a local hospital. I was getting stronger at each visit. I remember getting defiant with my sister at one of the visits. I don't know why. I think it was this intense need to remember things; acting as if there was nothing wrong with me - like I had not had a traumatic brain injury.

The survival rate for those with a ruptured brain aneurysm is about 60% (40% die). For those who survive and recover, about 66% have some permanent neurological defect. I can honestly say that I survived without any neurological defect. I will say that I now have problems adding and subtracting, but nothing that a calculator can't handle.

My memory is intact. I remember all things before and after the aneurysm. The event itself, I have no memory of. That is why I have asked my family and friends to fill in those events for me, which will be detailed in my upcoming book, "Sarah: An Aneurysm Survivor's Story".

My dad drove me everywhere I needed to go (medical, dental, follow-up appointments). I think it was around October when I felt comfortable driving again. I asked him to let me drive. So, that weekend he let me drive. For several weekends thereafter I was driving. By November, I was ready to be independent again. I was ready to live on my own. I rode home with him, because at the time, no one was leaving me by myself. I told him that I wanted to take my car back to my home. And, that I was not going to tell anyone that I would be staying by myself that weekend. He was okay with it, because he says that God speaks to us in different ways. I spent the weekend by myself. And that Monday, my sister came by. She was not pleased. She had been with me for months; the hospital, therapy, dental, and medical appointments. It was hard for her to let me go. I knew that everyone needed to get back to their lives. And, I needed to live again too.

I went for my 6-month check-up with the Neurologist. After several tests, I asked him if it was okay for me to go back to work. He told me that I could try. I did not know how to interpret that, so I asked my friend Jan. She said that he meant that I could try working; see how it feels; see how I will be able to handle it; work part-time hours for a month or so. So, I went back to work the first week of December in 2016. I worked 30 hours a week for a month. As I got, stronger, I went back to work in full-time status.

As of today, I still peer volunteer at the rehab hospital on the second and fourth Wednesday of each month. There are many times patients will pray with, and for me. I listen to their stories; *because everyone has a story*. I tell them what happened to me and the reason that I volunteer. Most are amazed because I don't look like what I have been through. I give them hope and inspiration. I let them know that they can do it. Just to take one day at a time. Because when you are hurt, you're vulnerable. You think of what you can no longer do for yourself. What you can no longer do for others. How they thought something was so important; but has little meaning now. Their whole focus now is directed toward healing. Oftentimes, I get more inspiration from them than they realize. I hope one day that they too, will become volunteers.

Thankful for My Dad

My Dad was turning 75 years old and I wanted to plan a memorable day for him. He has been by my side for many years. We have traveled together and went as far as West Africa. But, it was the time that he spent with me in the hospital and rehab that stood out for me. So, I wanted his day to be the most special. I contacted the caterer to help plan the menu. She agreed to give a taste test before receiving payment. I called the disk jockey, who happens to be my cousin. He said that he would not miss it for the world. I only had to pay for the gas to haul his equipment. The decorator was honored to help. She did not charge me for the event. She asked that I only pay for anything that she had to purchase. The photographer recorded his day in the most beautiful way. His event was in a park that had a small pond. Can you visualize the sun shining off the pond? It was amazing. My Dad had no idea that he was going to a surprise party. When he arrived at the venue and saw all the cars, I told him to act surprised. He had a beautiful day and a wonderful memory to cherish for the rest of his life.

The Itch Returned

The itch was back. And, it would not be ignored. It was during this time, that I really started to think about event planning as a business choice. In October of that year, I was invited to a friend's birthday party. She had called and asked if I would share with her guests how we met, how long we had known each other, and so forth. I agreed to do that. But, while I was sitting there waiting my turn to speak, other guests were telling us about how she had planned their family reunion. I began to have an "aha" moment. I remembered the times when she was planning family reunions. I knew that she was organized because we were both secretaries when we first met. She paid attention to detail. I thought, "O my God, I've found a partner." That night, I told her my vision for us. She agreed to call me the next day. Then, we became business partners.

The following Monday at work, I told a co-worker of mine about becoming an event planner. She told me that Atlanta Area Tech has an event planning course where you can get certified. When I got home that evening, I searched the website and found the course on Eventbrite. I immediately told my partner, and we both signed up for the course.

Empowered to Action

I was an attendee at Dr. Debra Wright Owen's (Dr. Debra), "Vision Emerge, Beyond the Vision Board". I encountered a God-filled woman who prophesized over my life. She asked each attendee what were they currently doing? What is it they wanted to do? What was there vision? I answered by saying that I was a Legal Support Coordinator in my profession. I had an aneurysm in 2016 and was on my second life. I made a list of things that I wanted to incorporate into my new life. I joined a kickball team to keep me active. I volunteered at the rehabilitation facility where I was a patient. I am a media specialist volunteer at the church that I attend. And, I had just started taking a certification course for events planning at a local technical college.

She listened to my responses and said to me, "I see you have an eye for detail. You see what others overlook. I prophesy that you have a future in staging." I was so taken aback because Dr. Debra had said to me on the Friday prior that staging was one of the things that I could or should do. I had not discussed anything with her about our conversation. And, here this woman was reinforcing that message. I was so empowered. I left the event with that at the forefront of my mind.

I had another engagement later that evening. I was reconnecting with a former co-worker whom I had not seen in 10 years. When I entered her living quarters, I was amazed. Everything had its place. Pops of color, candles, pillows, even a dedicated space for Prince (she is a true fan). I said to her, "I have a business proposal to run by you." I explained the encounter of what had happened less than 2 hours prior. I explained the prophecy that I had received earlier. I asked her to be my business partner. She instantly agreed. She said that she would help me any way that she could. Together we became R&R Stagers (Sarah **R**eid and Audrea **R**eynolds). Within the next few days, the federal government experienced a shutdown. During the down-time, I was able to create a website, establish a Facebook Business page and an Instagram account. I reserved our business name and applied for a Tax ID. We researched and created a business plan. R&R Stagers promoted their business through Facebook ads. We are eagerly anticipating our first client

In the meantime, my other friend and partner (Kathy Nelloms) became the Georgia Girls Event Planners. We have since earned a Certified Event Planner certification from Atlanta Area Technical College. We have created a Facebook and Instagram page to both, showcase our work and attract customers. I was at lunch one day with Dr. Debra and she mentioned offering tips for planning events. When I got back to the office, I contacted my partner and ran the idea by her. She thought it was a wonderful idea. So, together we came up with "10 Tips for Planning Your Holiday Event."

Soon after posting the Tips, I received a message from another reputable business owner wanting to enter a partnership. I was honored to be been asked. I shared the information with Dr. Debra and Sharon over lunch. They made me realize that it was a big deal to be asked. I thought, "Wow." I'm moving right along. I had contacted my partner earlier in the day and explained the message. She called me later that night and we reviewed the post together. We then decided on the response to her. I am so excited to know that we are moving forward on our vision to be entrepreneurs.

Where Vision Will Take You

When I attended Dr. Debra's *Vision Emerge* event in December of 2018, I had no idea that I would have progressed as far as I have. I am the co-creator of two businesses (R& R Stagers and Georgia Girls Event Planners). Initially, it did not start out that way. I knew about 25 years ago, that I wanted to start a business. I bought business books, one book in particular, "Starting a Home-Based Business". I remember going through the book, trying to determine what I was good at? What were my identified skills? As it turned out, my organizational skills and attention to detail propelled me into the industry of event planning and furniture staging.

What started out as a group of entrepreneurs getting together for a special event, has turned into a bond among eight women. Our ages range from 25 to senior. But that doesn't make us unique. What makes us unique is that we are all college-educated, and we bring something different to the table. We have a lawyer, mediator, financial advisor, event planner, crafter, graphic designer, and a coach in the mix. The respect that we have for one another, is unbelievable. Who do you know can be in a group of women, and everyone gets along? All we want is to see each other succeed. All things, no matter how small, are to be celebrated.

Dr. Debra is our coach and we were selected to participate in her pilot program. It's entitled, "Accelerate 90 Days". It is very informative because she provides you with the topic of discussion via text and email every Sunday night (for 90 days). She defines the terms that will be referenced, then poses questions that will apply to the topic and to us personally. I know this is a great deal of work because she had to prepare a lesson plan for each week. So, not only is she growing in her niche, but each of us are growing too. I think it was close to Week 4 when she sprung the idea about us being collective authors. I was in shock because I was already responsible for writing a book with a deadline. She told us that the proceeds from the sale of our collective work is to go to the "The Visionaire Foundation, Inc.," the nonprofit organization we created to give back to the community. The idea is to provide students with scholarships to assist with furthering their education. I love the concept. We have to support our children.

During our Vision Emerge Retreat in November, we selected board members for the foundation. I am still in awe of being a board member. I pinch myself and say, "I am a Board Member for the Visionaire Foundation." Things I did not expect. Things that I have a hard time wrapping my mind around. Dr. Debra always reminds me that anyone can do what is being done. Nothing is new. You just have to repackage it.

So, for right now, I am enjoying the ride. I am with women who have a purpose and a vision. I love each one of them. They have made me feel welcome, even with my alpha personality.

PART THREE

ADRIENNE GRAY

Life, Vision, Purpose AUTHOR SPOTLIGHT

Adrienne Gray

Founder of AEG Craft Designs (Handmade Home Designs)

Adrienne Gray retired as an IT Specialist with the federal government after accruing 34 years of service. She grew up in Pittsburgh, PA, and moved permanently to Atlanta, GA after graduating from Spelman College with a B.A. in English. Adrienne enjoys spending her time crafting, sewing, reading, and writing.

Beginnings

I am grateful to God to be here. I'm sure many of us say that when we wake up every day, but I'm sincerely grateful to have life.

I was born a couple of days after Thanksgiving. I wasn't supposed to be born until sometime in January. My mother thought she had indigestion, but she was in labor. I weighed a little over three pounds at birth. They kept me in the hospital until right around my actual due date. My mother says I was healthy so there was no reason to worry about my survival. This was in 1958 and I'm sure infant mortality was pretty high back then, but I made it. The mere fact that I survived has often made me wonder, why I am here. What's really my purpose?

I was born and raised in Pittsburgh, PA. I have a younger sister and we lived with both parents until I was about fifteen. I believe my mother tried to give us as normal a life as she could outside of what my father put her through. About my father; he was an alcoholic and physical abuser. He was not in the home for extended periods so, when he actually moved out my mother, sister and I were used to being on our own. We really didn't miss him.

I come from a family of creative, artsy people. My mother tells me when she was pregnant with me she searched for something to do with her hands. She said she once walked to a store in the snow to buy a coloring book. My father was not well educated, but he could draw. I remember him drawing characters from the comics section of the newspaper for my sister and me. My sister was part of a dance troupe in Pittsburgh and studied dance at the Boston Conservatory. My grandfather was a painter. He painted when he was young and put away his brushes to raise his family. After he retired, he went back to painting. Today, everyone in my family has at least one of his paintings in their house. He was also gifted at building things. He turned the basement of his house into a cozy family room. My grandmother and mother were seamstresses and my mother would sew a lot of our clothes. I remember handmade Halloween costumes and Easter outfits that were extraordinary. One year she made me a dress, coat and hat. She used the dress fabric for the lining of the coat. It was beautiful.

They introduced my sister and me to sewing early. My mom would give us her fabric scraps and we'd make clothes for our Barbie dolls. Sometimes we'd use thread and needle, but most times it was just about cutting holes for arms and heads. My grandmother was of the mind that young ladies should know how to do things like cook and sew. She sent my sister and me to sewing classes at Sears on Saturday mornings when I was about ten. By the time I was in high school I was a pro.

I loved to read and still do. I would walk to the local library and spend the day there. Throughout grade school reading or writing were favorite subjects. I also began writing poetry in grade school. I liked to draw. I would sit in front of the television and draw. If I didn't have a book in front of me while I watched television I would draw. I especially liked to watch Soul Train and draw the dancers' outfits. I also just liked to make things. In my day, they sent us to vocational school a few times a month to learn to use machines. This was in the seventh or eighth grade. I used saws and drills to make things with wood or metal. My mother still has many of the things I made in her home today.

When I got to high school I discovered I loved to write. I traded my sketch books for journals. My first high school English teacher had us start a journal. This is something I still do to this day. My outlet became poetry. I wrote about my life and what I wanted in my future. In the eleventh grade my English teacher encouraged my writing. This is also when I discovered I loved English literature and decided I wanted to be a writer.

I Always Wanted to Be a Southern Girl

When it came time to choose a college I knew I wanted to go to an HBCU. My mother told me I would need to stay close to home unless I got some type of financial aid. I remember researching Spelman and Morgan State. I believe it was an article in Ebony magazine that first made me aware of HBCU's and specifically Spelman. My mother thought I should go to a predominantly White school since I had gone to predominantly Black schools all my life. I knew I didn't want that. I also wanted to get out of Pittsburgh. Luckily, Spelman said yes and they offered enough financial aid and my mom said yes too. I had never been to Atlanta, but that's where I wanted to go; best decision of my life. When I look back at it now it was probably the best thing I ever did. I'm sure it hurt my mom that I moved so far away. But when I got to Atlanta I was amazed. I had never seen that many Black people together in one place. They were not just on campus. They were downtown. It was nothing like Pittsburgh and I loved it. Of course, I was homesick the first few weeks, but by Thanksgiving you couldn't pull me away.

I found myself at Spelman. I was on my own. Spelman presented me with people and experiences I had not been exposed to. I was not involved in a lot of things in Pittsburgh. Going away opened up a new world for me. I was with young Black people that had experiences and lives I never knew about. I made lifelong friends. I was an English major with a minor in Art. I loved my English classes. I wrote poetry that won prizes. I joined the English club and was active with the college's literary magazine. I flourished. My book was still in the back of my mind, but I didn't really think I could live on being a writer. I also had no clue what I would really write about.

After graduation, I decided not to go back to Pittsburgh. I searched for a job in advertising or journalism which was kind of difficult since I had no real world experience in either. So, my goal was to get any job. I got a job with the federal government and I ended up staying with the same agency for 34 years. I didn't intend to stay till retirement, but the job gave me good benefits and stability. I started out as a clerk typist, then a secretary. When I was about ten years in computers were introduced to my division and I was selected to learn all I could about them. Through self-teaching and offsite classes I learned enough to earn the title of Computer Assistant and then Computer Specialist and be made part of the Information Technology division. Thus, my "career" was born. Now, life would get in the way of any dreams I had and I let it. I met a man, got married and had children. I didn't write poetry. I didn't draw. I didn't sew. I really didn't even think about it. I was just living. I worked and took care of my family. I don't know where Adrienne with the dreams went.

Who Said This Would Be Easy?

My husband was 15 years older than me. That seemed to present some insecurity for him. He was twice divorced and had three children. I believed I would be his forever wife. After about five years of marriage we decided to have children. Unfortunately, I couldn't just get pregnant. I told myself that this was something a woman was supposed to just be able to do. If I couldn't what was my purpose? My husband was tested and all was well with him. I ended up having fertility treatments. No shots or surgeries. I was put on fertility drugs and had to track my periods.

I got pregnant. I was happy. He was happy. I was going to be a mom. We were going to be a family. This would be my legacy. Then, one night in my first trimester I went to the bathroom and heard something fall into the toilet before I got up. I looked at it and it wasn't bloody. I felt no pain. I don't know what I was thinking. I wasn't thinking. I flushed it. Then, I went to tell my husband to take me to the hospital.

They called it a spontaneous abortion. I had been pregnant, but clearly the fetus wasn't viable. Got the "you can try again" speech. I really heard nothing after they told me there was no baby. About a year later, we did try again and I got pregnant with the help of the drugs. We told no one and I walked on eggshells until I was out of the first trimester. I gave birth to a healthy daughter. Five years later we went through the same process and I had a son.

Now, I had a family and a home and I thought nothing of pursuing writing or of making things. I was someone's wife and mother and that's all there was. I clearly devoted most of my time to my children. I felt they needed me more than he did. I'm sure he began to feel left out.

There were always red flags in our relationship that I ignored. When we first got together I was kind of amazed that he thought other men were looking at me all the time. Towards the end of our relationship I was annoyed. I believed he chose alcohol over me. He controlled what I did. He didn't want me to travel or go very far without him or the children. My priority and purpose became being a good wife. I didn't leave him and I can't say why I didn't. I did still love him. I chose to stay with him and I chose to have children with him. When I had the children my priority and purpose was to be a good mother. I lost myself. We started having arguments. He constantly accused me of cheating on him. I wasn't. He told me he saw me in places I wasn't. He did things that he knew would hurt me emotionally. Through all of this I stayed with him. I told no one of our issues and lived with the constant degradation of my self-esteem; for better or for worse.

There are two sides to every story. When much of the child rearing was made my responsibility I did decide my children were more important than him. His drinking and possible drug use turned me off and I turned away. I loved him, but I didn't feel he loved me enough to stop. I also kept all that happened behind our doors to myself.

After living with outbursts, arguments and gas lighting for a few years I finally convinced him to visit a doctor. His behavior could not just be caused by drinking or drugs. Something else had to be going on. We found out he had prostate cancer. I went with him to doctor appointments and helped him with the treatments he had to have. He got a clean bill of health. Then, he decided he wanted to leave me. We had just moved into a new house. I called him to see what he was doing one day and he told me he was preparing to move out. I told him not to waste time and leave that day. It took him a month to move out. I was hurt and angry. Luckily, I was able to keep my house and let my children continue to live in the manner in which they had become accustomed; something I had learned from my mother. I was angry for almost ten years. Why? He didn't care. It was wasted energy for me.

Transitions

After my 50th birthday, I'd had enough of living in anger and I decided to try to live my golden life. I would walk from the parking lot to my office with Jill Scott singing "Golden" on repeat on my iPod. I started to write poetry again. I bought more journals and dedicated myself to posting every day. I was planning my retirement and I decided my life was going to be writing a book about my relationship. I was coming back to me.

In the meantime, my father died; the same day as Michael Jackson. I hadn't seen or talked to my father since I was 20. I was 51when he died. The last time I saw him I was working a summer job in Pittsburgh. When I got off the elevator on the way home one day, he was standing in the lobby. He worked maintenance in the building. We talked for a few minutes and I told him what was going on in my life. We planned to have dinner a few days later. The day of the dinner date he didn't show up and he didn't call. I went back to school in Atlanta. My mother told me she saw him some time later and asked him what happened. He told her he didn't show up because he didn't have anything to give me. She told him I didn't want anything, just some time. After his death I found out he named me as beneficiary for a final pension payment. It wasn't about the money, but it made me realize he did think of me. I know he had other children besides me and my sister, but

I think I was his oldest child. I split what he left me between my mother, sister and myself.

Not long after that, we found out my husband had bladder cancer. I went to doctor appointments with him. I sat through his chemo treatments and minor surgeries. He would call me when he needed to go to the emergency room and I'd take him. I was still married to him and he had no one else; in sickness and in health.

He died about six years after his diagnosis. I made his funeral arrangements and took care of all he left behind. I began to work on the book again. I can't say I was still angry with him but my anger and frustration came out in the pages. What I really felt about him was sympathy. I was questioned by family and friends why I did what I did for him. Why I was there for him. I can only say that he was still my husband; till death do us part.

Plans Made, Plans Changed

Now, my life would take another turn. I started working at a new office. I was talking to one of my new co-workers who asked me about my children. I told her I had a son and daughter. When she found out how old my daughter was she suggested I introduce myself to another co-worker with a daughter the same age.

I met Debra Owens in 2009. Her daughter was only a few days older than mine and her son was a few years younger than my son. She was a single mom and didn't live far from me. We had our children in common and a desire to do something that would not have us tethered to a government desk for eight hours.

I admired that she was working and taking classes toward a doctorate degree; something I could never see myself doing. Our talks mainly involved working our passion. We felt that we should be somewhere else doing something else making a living. We both made sure this was something we were also telling our children. Find your passion and work it. Don't be tied to a desk working for someone else. I am not a religious woman and she was and still is a spiritual advisor in my life.

At the time, my passion was writing. I would periodically work on the book I had dreamed of writing. I took a creative writing class at a nearby community center hoping for inspiration. It did help. Under the advisement of Debra and Sharon Gipson, I ended up starting a blog which I wrote for about two years.

I retired from my job of 34 years. That's what it was – a job. I never considered it a career. It's what paid my bills and fed my children. Since retiring, I have been searching for what I want to do with the rest of my life – my purpose. My sister told me my purpose was my children, but I always felt there was more than that. What was I going to do when they grew up and moved out? I needed to find something for me. I always tell my children to try to make their career something they love. Work your passion if you can. If it's what sustains you and pays your bills, that's even better. They were both beginning their search for what they would do in life. I decided to search for what I would do; what I loved.

After retirement, my original plan was to write books. The dream book I had been working on for years ended up being about three women of different generations and their experiences with domestic violence. I felt I could do something with this subject having lived through it with my parents and my husband. I wrote it. When I finished it I couldn't look at it anymore. I guess it was a therapy for me to get it out. I didn't want to see it anymore. I was done. Other ideas I had to write wouldn't come either. I honestly tried to write, but nothing really came to me.

Cooking had become somewhat therapeutic for me. I'd spend the day watching chefs on cooking channels learning new techniques. I learned a lot and tried new recipes on my family. One of my former roommates and I even talked about putting together our own cookbook.

Debra called me in December 2018 for her first Vision Emerge empowerment luncheon. I was one of seven women she had chosen to participate. We were all to define our vision and work towards achieving it. It was suggested to me that I combine my love of cooking and writing and work on a cookbook. I thought about it, but that wasn't where I wanted to go at the time.

I continued to jump around in finding my passion, my purpose. Then, I was invited to join a crafting group on

Facebook. The women I saw in the group inspired me to try new crafts and to return to some things I was already familiar with. I always liked making things and creating. I decided to sew and make things for my home. I also saw that many of the women in the crafting group were actually making money with their crafts. They were turning their hobby into a business. I could do that! I had found my place.

In the year since that initial meeting I have sold Christmas wreaths and placemats. I am looking to selling at a craft fair. Our group has also formed The Visionaire Foundation, Inc. We are a nonprofit that plans to offer financial assistance to students needing help. These women have become a source of empowerment and inspiration for me. I love that we're all different, but we're the same.

I Got This!

I continue to define and search for my purpose. Perhaps part of it was to raise two responsible, caring people. I sometimes think I am here to be an ear for certain people in my life. I may not always have answers for them, but I listen when they need me. Sometimes that's all they need.

I enjoy the making things and being creative part of my life. That's just my passion and what makes me happy. In my life I've tried woodworking, needlepoint, knitting, pottery, painting, drawing and sewing. Maybe my mom needing to use her hands when she was pregnant with me became part of me. If I can make someone else happy by creating something for them, I want to do it. I've found my true passion in sewing.

I've also come to realize I need to love and take care of me first. I think I tried to be everything for everyone. I don't know that anyone really noticed that I sometimes needed help. I guess I hid it well. I truly felt I was doing the right thing for my husband when he got sick. We were still married regardless of what he had put me through. My purpose was to be a good wife. I thought nothing of any dreams I once had. His accusations and disrespect did wear me down. I should have stood up and taken action in some way other than striking back. I can blame no one but myself. As Bernadine said in the movie "Waiting to

76

Exhale", I became the background to his foreground. I never want to be that woman again. If I have to choose defining moments in my life the first would be going to Spelman, the second deciding to let go of anger and helping my husband and the third becoming involved with the Visionaires.

I have specifically been searching for what I want to do in my life since retiring. When my interest in my book fell short I had no idea of what to do. I never saw myself doing what I am now. I feel I am actually acting on my vision. At times, I am hesitant and apprehensive about any gift I may have. I am plagued with self-doubt, but I really try to get past it and step out. I have told my children to step out on faith and follow their dreams. Who am I to tell them to follow their dreams when I'm not doing it myself? I want to be an example to them and let them see I'm practicing what I preach. I think they have both stepped out a little in their passion. My daughter has found her gift in makeup and making wigs. My son has created his own clothing line.

There's a question I remember being asked very often when I would go on job interviews. Where do you see yourself in 5 years? Right now, I hope to be "happily crafting". I plan to make it a real business. I want to get my sewing back to where I was in high school and college. Right now, I'm still in my comfort zone. I'm working on stepping out more and not treat what I do as a hobby. Maybe I'll even actually finish and publish that book. I really hope to look back and ask myself what I was afraid of.

PART FOUR

BEVERLY VANN-WOODS

Life, Vision, Purpose AUTHOR SPOTLIGHT

Beverly Vann-Woods

Founder of Woods Mediation Services, LLC

Beverly Vann Woods is a native Tennessean that has called Atlanta home for the past 35 years. Shortly after moving to Atlanta, Beverly began work for the Internal Revenue Service and has over 33 years of federal experience in the areas of Human Resources, Organizational Development, EEO, Negotiations and Mediations. With a Master of Science in Human Resource Management, State Certifications in Mediation and Arbitration, Beverly is well equipped and uses her engaging, and communicative style to help resolve disputes in the workplace. Beverly's biggest joy by far comes from her love of family and friends and her desire to see everyone succeed and be the best version of themselves. Beverly uses her personal triumphs and tragedies to serve as a beacon of hope in a very challenging world.

Beginnings Do Not Determine Endings

It's funny how life's circumstances will force you to reflect on things you'd long since forgotten. As a child we are often asked and dream about what we want to be when we grow up. Somehow in the process of growing up, what you want to be and what you become are not always in sync. Childhood dreams and visions are based on the limited life experiences that we have up until that point. Needless to say, many of the dreams and wishes included toys, ice cream and all the candy you could find. As we grow older our dreams turn to vanity in being concerned with how good we look, how popular we are and how many friends we claim to have. Our young adult years find us thinking and wondering what path our future will take; how much money we will make and who we will marry. Like most others, I too experienced the dreams of grander. For the most part, my childhood was pretty standard in comparison to that of my childhood friends. We shared much of the same family makeup and all had strong ties with our grandparents as extended family members. In some ways though, I was different from a few of my close friends, since I was raised by a single mom and they had both parents in the home. Although I had many surrogate dads by way of my uncles, there was always that little empty feeling of not having a biological dad present. If I am to be truthful, the absence of a father shaped many of my decisions and actions into adulthood. I did know who my biological father was, however, I never had a relationship with him. Although, his absence did not prevent me from reaching goals and making achievements, the notion of "daddy issues" is real. No matter how great the substitutes are, there is always a nagging feeling of insecurity and longing to know why. As a parent with the deep resounding love I have for my children, I could never imagine not having a relationship with them. However, being the mediator that I am, I do try to look at both sides of an issue. In defense of my biological father, I have no clue of who his role models were. No clue of what childhood issues he experienced, or any type of trauma endured. However, I also subscribe to the fact that it could be that he was just a self-absorbed being, that didn't want his life interrupted by the inconvenience of an unplanned child. Whatever the case, since he is no longer alive, these are things I will never know. Reflecting through the pages of my memory bank, the most profound memory is the last and only verbal conversation I had with him. After reaching 50 and still experiencing the whispering echoes of daddy issues, I decided to reach out to this person to find out why they had chosen not to play that role in my life. Sadly, after summoning the courage to reach out to him, I was unfortunate enough to catch him in an inebriated state seemingly void of any clear thinking. Rather than convince him that it was I, the abandoned child, now 50-year old women seeking closure, I chose to let him think I was someone playing a prank on him. In his liquored state, this explanation was something he could believe, rather than the raw truth. While initially angry for allowing myself to reach out to him, I realized that it was actually very enlightening and therapeutic. The fact is that we are all responsible for our own decisions in life and how we choose to address them. I have learned that others are not always capable of giving us what we want from them. The expectations sometimes simply cannot or will not be met.

Not as Planned

After completing a college degree and moving to the Black Mecca a.k.a. Atlanta, my life began to unfold in ways I had not planned. A couple of years after moving, I found myself as a single parent at 25 with a daughter. This was certainly not the fairytale I had imagined. Nevertheless, I was determined to keep my promise I made. My daughter would know her father and he would be in her life, regardless to our situation, no daddy issues for her. Turns out things didn't work between her dad and I, however, but she avoided the experience of not having a dad in her life. She ended up with two dads as a matter of fact, as my husband has been in her life since the age of five.

As dreams collide with real life, you realize that dreams often can and will fail to materialize the way you had hoped. Reflecting, I remember dating what seem to be prominent men, who would have been considered "a good catch" however it never seemed to work out. Hmmmm… Some of those "good catches" are not doing so good today. God works in mysterious ways. You may be asking how this could have anything to do with God's work. I too, often question his works that have occurred over the past 59 years of my life. But for you bible scholars, the word says we are wonderfully and fearfully made. God knows the number of the very hairs on our head. One thing for sure that I have learned on this life's journey, is that nothing "just happens". I have learned that all things work together, and more importantly, that during my life, all roads traveled have led me here today.

Chosen from the Beginning

Writing this chapter on being chosen and how my attempt to navigate the many decisions in my life have led me to the pages of this book, is what I am attempting. But wait, I am getting ahead of myself. As a believer, I know that my life from the beginning has been known and formed for me, even before I had a choice to decide. As they say, there is nothing that surprises God; He is the alpha and the Omega, the beginning and the end! What we are today can be revealed through looking back at those small subtle events that shaped our beginning. As I stated earlier, my beginning was not what I would have dreamed it to be.

Don't get me wrong I was fortunate in that I come from a very loving immediate and extended family and there was no shortage of love shown to me from that circle. As a matter of fact, my mother is one of my biggest supporters and my maternal grandmother was my special angel until she passed away. I was always that special baby girl; clearly my mom and grandma's favorite. (Shush, don't tell the others) Being the special one, I soon learned was a blessing but also a curse. The bar for success is always set high and expectations always higher. The "one" is expected to succeed and set the example for others. I remember my grandmother's reaction when I had my first child out of wedlock. She let me know that she was hurt and disappointed; not for me being unmarried and having a child, but because she had hopes for me and expected me to make better choices. Her disappointment would drive me to ensure that I would have a husband the next go round. Feeling like I was "chosen" even back then was something I couldn't grasp the depth of what it meant. Why did it seem that expectations were always different for me and not others? Why did I have to set the example? Why did I have to finish college? So many why's filled my life as I continued to search for the answers. I still find myself searching through the why's of life.

On the road to purpose the whys often continue. Why me? Why am I that parent with the troubled child... that spouse who bears the brunt of the marriage AND the one who has to compromise. Maybe you are that employee who has to pick up the slack for your coworkers, that one responsible child that the parent looks to and counts on to make sure the family is taken care of. WHY ME??????

Why me Lord? I remember the elders in the church singing "Why me Lord". The answer is as complex as it is simple. The simple answer is that you like me were chosen. Chosen to live a life that was predestined, pre-determined before the foundations of the world. Ephesians 1:4 says "he hath chosen us in him before the foundation of the world that would be holy and without blame before him in love". We are again reminded in Jeremiah 1:5 that the Lord knew us long before he formed us. "Before I formed thee in the belly, I knew thee and before thy camest forth out of the womb, I sanctified thee, and I ordained thee a prophet unto the nations." For those of us who are believers, we must know that the Omnipotent all-knowing power of God is just that. And if we believe, then we know that it was not an accident or coincidence that we are born into the family that we were meant to be. You had the children that were destined to be yours and that you were meant to parent; the spouse you were meant to have. Nothing surprises God, and nothing comes to pass that he doesn't allow. It is we that must understand that we are chosen for purpose and are assigned to fulfill that purpose or purposes as determined by God. To be chosen and fulfill your purpose is the greatest accomplishment you can have in life. It is not how much money we make or fame we achieve, but how well we fulfill our purpose.

Purpose in the Pain

Coming into this reality has helped me to navigate through the sorrow from losing my son, which still is the most difficult thing I have had to face. Recognizing, acknowledging and walking in purpose allowed me also to stay married during the difficult times. You know those for "better or worse times" that you say as you excitedly recite your vows. Never knowing how bad the worse will be. Remember you prayed for that man to be your spouse and sometimes although God will give you the desires of your heart, it seems as if he throws in a little extra. You may ask, "wait God, I don't remember asking for that, why did you have to add to my desire?" Often, we become frustrated when questions seem to go unanswered or event worse when the answer is "My grace is sufficient". It is then you really realize the gravity of that assignment and the weight of the vows you took. My prayer for you (you will know if this is directed to you) is that whether you are still in that relationship or not, you are able to recognize that you were chosen for that season. It is when you really deeply search within, that you realize that you are chosen.

The realization doesn't necessarily mean that the marriage partner you picked was not your equally yoked spiritual partner that God ordained for you. What it does mean is that you were meant to pour into and give purpose to that person that you have joined with in matrimony. Even if your marriage is only for a brief season, I am a firm believer that it was chosen to be for that time. A relationship chosen for a purpose. While walking in purpose, the way and how are sometimes not clear. The bible talks about "in due season". In due time you will come to realize that you were meant for the appointed time, so that you could do the will of the Lord. Not our will but his will be done.

Searching Through the Pain

My biggest challenge to accept regarding purpose was my most recent and heart-breaking challenge. Trying to understand God's glory and purpose after losing my only son in a fatal car accident. My 27-year-old prince whose absence still causes my heart to break each day. The pain of that never ends, only subsides enough to get through the day. What could possibly be the purpose in that? Hadn't I gone through enough raising him to get him to the place where his dad and I could finally breathe a sigh of relief? We had survived the elementary years with the diagnosis of ADHD, the teen age years of low self-esteem and anger issues; even his reaching 18 and being pulled over by the police on more than one occasion simply for

DWB (Driving while black). We survived all of that, all while recognizing and nurturing the creative God-given talent that he naturally possessed. Breathing a sigh of relief after our son reached 25, the turning point for most young men. The age when they realize that they are getting older and their outlook on life begins to turn toward a more mature way of thinking. In the year or so leading up to his death, my son began a spiritual journey and began in-depth study of religion. He spent countless hours reading and researching various biblical sources in his search for his truth. He became very passionate about pleasing God and even more passionate that his family did the same. He also had great hopes of bringing his various writings, scripts and monologues to life. As I reflect on all the money spent nurturing and developing his skills, time spent in endless hours of communications assuring him of his talents, sacrificing to make sure he didn't become another young black male lost to violence - those times when he would experience depression and withdraw angrily or dwell in solitude. After coming through all these seemingly insurmountable obstacles, with hope flourishing in the thought that our son was well on his way to succeed, he had finally overcome. The hope tragically diminishing no sooner than it had been realized in a sudden tragic turn of events - without explanation or warning; it was all over. As parents, we were left with the pain, anguish, anger and unanswered questions. Yet somehow, there was supposed to be purpose; purpose in the pain?

I Didn't Know this God

My relationship tested with the loving God I had been taught to fear and love; the God who is all knowing and my protector - and the Lord of my life and my family. This God, who now was seemingly an unfair and unjust father; whose comfort I could not find. The God whose wisdom I could not understand and actions that I could not comprehend. At one point I asked out loud, Why God? Why would you take my son, he was my only son? It was then that the Lord spoke to me and said He understood, "…He (Jesus) was my only son". I had to send him into a world and have him become a living sacrifice. You see my child; the world took my son at an early age as well. At 33 years old Jesus was crucified. But you are Lord, you allowed it to happen. I couldn't see why God would speak such words to me when I was looking for satisfaction and answers about my son. The words about his son, although very profound, did not provide the comfort to my aching heart that I was longing for. The Lord then further spoke to me and imparted the wisdom of his actions. God said, "I chose you to watch over one of my greatest creations and to be his mother so that he could fulfill my purpose. I chose you because no one else could love him, cherish him, nurture him and help prepare him for me like you could. No other mother in all the universe could form the bond I ordained for you and him to share. I called him home because he was ready to return to me. I know that you were not ready, but you had fulfilled my purpose. You were not ready, but he was ready. My ways are not your ways; my thoughts are not your thoughts. Daughter, please take comfort in knowing you fulfilled that purpose that I called you for. Although your heart is broken and the hurt you feel will never completely leave, "My grace is sufficient."

My mind then began to reflect on a very profound conversation I had had with my son a few months earlier. My son said that he had been chosen to share God's word with his family and friends. He went on to say that he didn't know why he was chosen. Of course, at the time, I thought my son was just talking and trying to convince me that I needed to listen to him and stop watching the television. If only I had known, I would have. As God would have it, while my son was talking, I took out my phone and began to record him. I am forever grateful that I made that recording. It has been through listening to his words and reflecting on the revelation made to me by God, I finally understand that everything was for purpose. Purpose, even thru the pain and feelings of despair.

Revelations through the Pain

Later, as I begin to seek more understanding, God revealed that being my son's mother was just one of my assignments of purpose that he had for me. Other assignments were also chosen specifically for me. Chosen to be the sister to my brother during his illness, chosen to be the wife to my husband during his bout with throat cancer, chosen to hold my friend's hand in prayer and hope for the desired diagnosis to be revealed. God needs each of us to be on assignment for those things which he specifically chose us for. God let me know that he wouldn't have chosen me if he didn't first equip me with the strength and grace to complete the task. God knows that we see many of these assignments for which we are chosen as burdens, but they are really assignments entrusted to you because you are the best person to handle them. While going through does not feel good and often seems more than we can bear, we must know that we were uniquely equipped and designed for the task as we were chosen. A purpose for the up-building of the kingdom; but rest assured that God will never leave you or forsake you. You may find yourself as I did, becoming discouraged, angry and refusing to accept his ways, but he never leaves us. He said it in his word that he would never leave or forsake us. And although at time it doesn't seem to be the case, it is truly an honor to be chosen. Matthew 22:14 says that "Many are called, but few are chosen". As part of the chosen few, you have been set aside to serve me. How wonderful to be chosen; a true honor to be called. Matthew 7: 13-14, says that the gate is narrow, and the way is hard that leads to life, therefore few are chosen. The thing about being chosen is that, depending on the assignment, the life as we know it can be dramatically changed. The conversations with God about being chosen to parent my deceased son, is a never ending one. Each day comes with new questions, new pains, new mercies and new revelations. Maybe in part because no matter how many revelations I get, the pain never completely subsides. The pain that changes from day to day, will not let me forget the plans and desires I had for my son. Although I have a better understanding of the pain and the purpose, many days I can't seem to get past it. The pain seems to override the purpose. The pain clouds the vision, although at times it subsides just enough for me to acknowledge that I was chosen. I still find myself in reflection over the 27 years with my son and how much life was packed in that short period of time. The many conversations, his revelations he received from God and his love and zeal not only for his family but all those he encountered still makes my heart smile. The bond that we had, which at times I thought would overwhelm me, now gives me some solace in that I know not all mothers and sons get to share that type of bond. But still I am haunted by the wife he will never marry, the children he will never have, the legacy I thought he would leave. As I said earlier, while I do understand that I was chosen, the painful "what ifs" never leave. Through my reflections, I am reminded that there is a strange irony that in one of my last conversations with him, he spoke of being chosen to help save his family. One of the biggest truths I have discovered through this pain filled purpose, is that I likely would not have searched for my Godly purpose with as much intent had my son still been alive. I never understood why he was so adamant about having spiritual and scriptural discussions with me daily. How he told me he couldn't stop talking and sharing because the Lord had chosen him although he didn't know why. During the final months of his life, he seemed to become more obsessed with fulfilling his purpose and making sure his family would be saved. He would make me promise to read certain biblical teachings and to consider changing things he said were not in line with what God ordained, such as eating pork and not fully observing the sabbath. He shared with me that he struggled with why God had chosen him, but then he later learned to accept it. I didn't know it at the time, but he was preparing me for the acceptance of being chosen. Coming to the revelation that my son was chosen and had begun to accept his assignment, which meant he would leave me, is something that has proven difficult. While my spiritual mind understands it, my physical pain as a mourning mother struggles to get past it. I can almost hear my son say, "Mom, it's because you are thinking with your emotions and not seeing the vision. These words cause me to reflect on Jesus' words to his mother Mary that he had to be about his father's business. During my times of frustration with my son's insistence on intense daily conversations that were held during the time of my favorite evening television shows. He would sometimes become frustrated with my lack of attention and hearing me say "I can hear you" as I struggle to read the subtitles of the closed caption I had secretly turned on. As I think now, of course if given another chance, I would gladly give all the time and attention to him that I could find. Unfortunately, that's not how life works. What seemed annoying would be a welcomed blessing to me now. As life continues to move forward, I slowly begin to realize that I was fulfilling one of my assignments. As I mentioned earlier, I recorded my son during one of his times of spiritual revelation. I felt compelled to record his "message". My thought was to play it back later so I could really "hear" what he was saying. Little did I know this simple act would turn out to be an eternal recorded message from my son to his family and friends; that would literally change lives. The seventeen-minute recording of love and revelation would serve as his legacy and roadmap to share with family and friends. A moment etched in time that I am forever grateful the Lord allowed me to capture and share. I wasn't aware of the impact and importance, but of course God knew. I thank God for allowing me to continue to walk in this parenting purpose by sharing with the world this message. One of my next acts will be to publish that seventeen-minute message, because I am confident someone will hear it and received the relation it was meant to give. I was chosen to be a mother of a young prophet and trusted by God to share the word and message to the reader, hearer and doer of his word. I join in my son's prayer that family and friends will be blessed and come into the full knowledge of God. This is also a prayer I have for myself as I continue to encourage other "chosen" parents to recognize that God chose you for your family and trust you to do what no one else can do.

Vision

We all know that the journey to any destination starts with the first step. What is your first step to reaching your purpose, your vision, walking in what God has designed and directed for you? Taking a moment, no make that several moments, to look at your life and reflect on what your legacy will be; what you were created to do during the time here and figuring out how to move forward in vision, can be a daunting task. I sincerely believe that whatever decision you make regarding vision must be tied to purpose. They must be indelibly woven together to create the abundant life that God wants for us. Even more challenging, can be trying to determine what steps are required to getting there. Reflecting on my life and what I have thought to be some of my greatest purposes (yes there is more than one, although parenting my son ranks high), I look forward to press toward the mark of the high calling. I keep the words before me that your vision is directly tied to your purpose. As a chosen wife, mother, daughter, sister and friend, my vision is to be able to walk in all those roles with authority, ability, confidence, capability and effortless excellence. To operate in the spirit of excellence in every endeavor is what I seek. My vision before me includes philanthropy that allows me to pour into family, friends and strangers in a way that has a lasting and meaningful impact in their lives. I pray to be able to do so and rejoice out of the abundance of giving and making a difference. I look forward to becoming the lender and not the borrower, being the head and not the tail, walking in purpose with the divine fruits and financial ability to do so without fear or restrictions. I thank God for allowing me to flow in my God given talents and abilities with ease and create a wealth and revenue stream that will allow me to do so. I recognize that to do so will require faith and action on my part. I will be required to launch out into the deep and make hard decisions which will require me to trust God. As I get closer to jumping off into the unknown, I am sometimes overcome with uncertainty fear and doubt. As a federal employee of almost 33 years, I have been fortunate to reach a level of financial success in my current position. I know that I would not be able to fully walk in my purpose without the blessing of having a career with the government, but still it is not my divine purpose. It did serve its purpose to allow me to take this next step. While I am not telling anyone to quit their job, I do recognize the limitations that come with my job and how they have to be removed in order to truly operate in my purpose. The bible speaks of not being able to serve two masters, for you will love one and hate the other. The feeling of being pulled into my purpose and vision causes me to like my government job less and less. The financial security is a shackle that has kept me in voluntary servitude. I often question whether my faith is in line with my zeal to fulfill my purpose. Seemingly not. I say seemingly because to admit this means I am inadvertently limiting God. Being ruled by the doubt and fear that I cannot sufficiently maintain my comfortable life is a trick of the enemy, but one that finds its way frequently entering my mind space. In the contrast, walking by faith means I am confident that God will supply all my needs above all I can ever hope or think. Sounds good right? As you see, getting the mind, body soul and spirit on the same page is essential in moving forward into purpose. Overcoming the spirit of fear is a real first step into overcoming and walking into victory. I am committed to moving forward with favor and victory. I recently decided that the upcoming year 2020 would be my last year working as an employee with the federal government and I would submit my retirement papers. Friends and family while happy for me, let me know of their apprehension. Because we have been conditioned to think that in order to be assured success, we must work "for someone" rather than be the leaders we are called to be. We are taught to get the job, work until we are no longer physically able and then retire to sit on the front porch in our rockers until the Lord calls us home. This is what we have been taught "success" is. We are taught to be cautious of dreaming bigger and taking risk and daring to step out. It is said that as a man or woman thinks so are, they, which is why transforming your mind is a first step to achieving greatness and walking in excellent purpose. I remind my family and friends that retirement from a corporate job does not mean retiring from life or success. It very well could and for me does mean retiring from the limitations that are preventing me from living that purpose filled vision and God blessed life that will allow me to abundantly bless others as well. I am often reminded of a vision God showed me over 20 plus years ago. I am on a stage in a large venue with a massive audience listening intently as I speak and pour into them. The scene reminds me of "ted talks" that I have seen on television. That vision will remain until I have fulfilled it. You know what they say, name it and claim it! But they also say, faith without works is dead. Ask yourself, what is it that is keeping you from finding your purpose or taking your first step toward vision. Recognizing the need to leap to land into purpose is something that I cautiously ask you to consider as well. It is with excited trepidation that I look forward to fulfilling that vision and sharing the message. I remember looking pretty good on that stage, so I am also claiming and thanking God for the good health that he will provide. Removing limitations is the start to living life and requires us to introspectively examine ourselves. My vision is limitless with limitless possibilities for success and operating in excellence. The only thing standing between you and success is "movement". I recently mentioned to my daughter that the only difference between those other people in the gym losing weight and getting in shape is "movement". Getting movement in the right direction in a consistent and steady manner is imperative to reaching any goal. Again, starting with the mind, which in turn controls the body and sets forth the movement to succeed. No matter what the vision or the task, you will be required to move and continue to move again and again. As the end of another year draws near and many reflect on the challenges, disappointments and heartache that it brought, I am thankful to God that I also am reflecting on the limitless possibilities that God has lain before me. I am grateful that he will allow me to succeed at whatever I put my hand forth to do. I am grateful that he will allow me to operate in a spirit of excellence. I am grateful for the opportunity to be a philanthropist and motivation to others. I am grateful for the great health and strength that he will afford me to accomplish all that is before me. I am excited about the growth and success not only for me, but those around me.

I am excited to have come into the knowledge and meaning of my chosen purposed life. While there are still many days where I feel sadness, loneliness and anxiety of what has gotten me to this point, I am excited for what God has in store for me. I am thankful for the favor and abundant blessings that he has before me and the provisions to achieve my visions. I pray not only for success, but that my success is a blessing to others. I am grateful to know that favor and blessings are not only for me and my family to enjoy, but we are blessed to be a blessing to others. Even in my son's death, he is still blessing others which still astonishes me as I write the closing words. I am thankful that the Lord has chosen us for a greater purpose and made provision to accomplish those things. I pray that all reading my words in this book would be encouraged and motivated to reflect on your chosen life, your purpose and your vision to move forward. Don't be afraid to think outside the box, outside the norm of what the world, family and friends have told you is your safe and what a certain path to success should be. 1 Corinthians 2:9 states that "But it is written, Eye hath not seen, nor ear hared, neither have entered into the heart of man, the things which God hath prepared for them that love him". If you love God, sometimes your path takes you down paths that you don't understand and can't even imagine to be. Having faith that if he gives you a vision and purpose to fill, he will also make provision to accomplish what is set forth before you. As my pastor often says, having faith to trust him (God) during the time when you can't trace him, requires faith. In closing I wish for all my family, friends, love ones and all those that I encounter that we would all prosper, but more importantly that our souls also prosper. Take time to look deeper into your life, pray for guidance on determining your purpose. After seeking God or just discovering from him, what your purpose should be, begin to work on a vision to help you reach your destination. Continue to pray and ask for guidance and strength even in those dark times when you can't see how there could possibly be purpose in the pain.

PART FIVE

SHARON GIPSON

Life, Vision, Purpose AUTHOR SPOTLIGHT

Sharon Gipson

Founder of Sew Recreative, LLC

Sharon Gipson is an attorney with over thirty years of professional experience as a litigator, mediator, and arbitrator. She has a heart for volunteerism and has served her community in several capacities over the years. In her spare time, Sharon loves to indulge in arts and crafts.

Life is What You Make It

I am the younger of two siblings. When I was young, our family lived in New York state. We moved to Georgia when I entered the first grade. I grew up in the small town where my father was born and raised.

I had a fantastic childhood. Our parents adored us and freely gave us their time, attention, and so many wonderful opportunities. I am convinced that our parents knew the value of the experiences they shared with us. They raised us intentionally. I was in all kinds of clubs and activities throughout my school years. I loved music and art (still do!). I took piano lessons and played in the band in high school. I had wonderful friends. I got to travel and spend time with family. I was blessed with a great upbringing.

I loved my college years (my HBCU is Jackson State University, Jackson MS). I made lifelong friends, did great academically, pledged Delta Sigma Theta Sorority Inc., and I was involved in all sorts of clubs and activities. I learned so much during my college years and grew into

111

an adult during that season. The knowledge and support that I gained at JSU prepared me well for the educational and life experiences that were to come.

I wanted to be closer to home for graduate school, so I chose Emory University School of Law in Atlanta, GA. After graduating from Emory, I went to work in the Atlanta area. I have been practicing law for over thirty years. Currently I work as a labor and employment lawyer.

Like everyone, I have had some setbacks and disappointments in my life: I have lost family members and friends, I experienced a divorce, I have had professional disappointments, but these kinds of things happen to all of us. No one is immune to real life. Despite all these things, I am truly blessed to be living a good life, and even though I am blessed and things are good, it does not mean that I am sitting back satisfied and content. No Ma'am, No Sir.

I am a woman in my fabulous fifties who is consistently striving to live my best life. What do I mean by that?

Honestly, there is really no one response to that question because living my best life varies depending on what I am doing, where I am, and how I feel. However, there are some consistent features to "living my best life": I need to be doing things I love around people that I love (or at least like), I need to use my gifts and abilities to help people, and I need to take care of myself in the process. I do not always meet all those requirements at the same time, but I am trying pretty much all the time. That is why I say that I am <u>striving</u> to live my best life.

I have not always been intentional about living my best life. I can see that so clearly when I look back over the years. In my younger adult years, when I was twenty something and thirty something, I focused on my creating a rewarding personal life and developing in my career. That sounds like a good thing, right? However, in retrospect, I can see how I often failed to prioritize the critical factors of the "living my best life" formula that I talked about above. I did not always make sure that I was doing things I loved around people that I loved (sometimes I did not even like the people I was around). I often disregarded my gifts and abilities, and I put my self-care on the back burner. Honestly, self-care was sometimes not even a consideration as I was focusing on "other attentions". I worked hard, I enjoyed my life, and I am currently benefitting personally and professionally from many of the choices that I made during those years. However, I am also <u>recovering</u> from some of the choices that I made (and failed to make) during those years.

Deciding to Put "Me" First

I am recovering from years of practicing the bad habit of failing to look out for myself as fiercely as I should have. I have an innate desire to take care of others and to make sure that everyone and everything is alright. That is not a bad thing, in fact is it an admirable quality in my opinion. However, there must be a balance between caring for others and caring for self. Self-care is not just important. It is critical to survival.

There were times when I worked despite being physically sick and mentally exhausted. I have cancelled or postponed medical appointments because I "had" to take care of someone or something. In the past, I have cancelled vacations and simple days off (mental health days) in favor of the needs (wants?) of others. I have worked to the point of exhaustion, and then I would come home to care for our home. I skipped engaging in hobbies and activities that I loved in order to be available for events and sometimes people that did not really require or deserve my presence. For a time, I was existing as a human-doing instead of living as a human being.

I started realizing there was a problem with how I was prioritizing my life some time in my thirties- a long time before I actually started doing anything about it. There is not one particular event that caused me to realize that I had a problem and that I needed to change. Instead, over time I just got tired of generally not feeling well and getting sick with classic stress symptoms. My body was suffering in ways that scared me, so I was forced to seek medical attention. I didn't just go because I needed to go- I was <u>forced </u>to get real. If you do not take care of yourself willingly, you <u>will</u> take care of it out of necessity.

I am so grateful that I did not suffer a heart attack or stroke, cancer or other serious health challenge that so many women, especially Black women, suffer because we don't stop and take care of ourselves.

Out with the Old, In with the New

So yes, I am a woman in my fabulous 50's striving to live my best life. Learning to prioritize myself has been an undertaking that has been more difficult than I would have ever expected. It is an ongoing effort. My prayer for everyone, including myself, is that we all figure out how to live our best lives, and having done the work to figure it all out, we consistently make it happen.

It is not easy to consistently live your best life. I am definitely not suggesting that it is a simple task. That is why I admit that I am striving to do it every day. There are many obstacles. One of the biggest obstacles to living your best life is the way we think – our habits and beliefs. We all have habits/beliefs that, if they ever really served us, certainly do not serve us now.

It is hard to break old habits and beliefs because they are ingrained in us. Scripture says that we should stop being conformed to the world, and instead be transformed by the renewing of our minds. Sadly, we simply don't follow these instructions. Most of the time we do things we have always done with no real understanding of the "whys" of our behavior, and no real analysis as to whether the habits and beliefs are actually benefiting us. We mindlessly conform and avoid doing the work to be transformed. It is really easy to just keep doing what you are doing, but when old ways no longer serve us, or actually become destructive, we have to stop, ask ourselves some hard questions, and do the work to be transformed.

The hard questions that can lead to transformation are actually simple questions. The hard part is making ourselves provide honest answers. The transformation questions include, "why am I doing this?", "is this benefitting me (or anyone)?", "why am I afraid to do something different, and is that a realistic fear?", "what's the worst that can happen if I do (or don't do) that?" Our habits and beliefs may be serving us, and if so, that fact will be revealed when these simple questions are answered. However, if our habits and beliefs are not serving us, that too will be revealed.

We can begin the process of breaking old habits and discarding beliefs that are no longer useful if we honestly answer these questions. Then we can create new habits and beliefs that can help us as we strive to live our best lives. This process is not something that we have to do by ourselves. A coach, therapist, counselor, or a trusted friend can assist with the process of facing and providing honest answers to these questions about our habits and belief, especially if we recognize that the habits and beliefs are no longer serving us, but have difficulty facing and addressing this fact.

Another major obstacle to living our best lives can be the company we keep. Our friends and family can keep us stagnant, or they can have us upset and unfocused, if we allow. Conversely, keeping the right people in your circle can help you stay motivated, focused, and on the right track.

Watch the Company You Keep

When I was growing up, I remember that my parents were always interested in who my friends were. Not only did they want to know who they were, they wanted to know their parents, where they lived, what they did, all sorts of things that I thought were just extra nosy and intrusive (smile). I remember once they would not allow me to go on a date with a boy they did not know and I could not make them know his family! That is so funny now, but back then I was MAD. As an adult, I know that their interest was way more serious than I could have ever guessed. Our friends and associates really matter. And the friends and associates of our friends, and our dates and potential mates, really matter. Our friends can put us in mortal danger simply because of what they do and who they hang around with, so it is imperative that we choose our friends wisely. We must ask (yet another set of) hard questions about our friends and associates, and we MUST pay attention to the answers. What do they do, what kind of people do they associate with, what are their habits, what are their relationships with others like, do they have good reputations, how do they treat other people, what are their beliefs?

In addition to impacting our physical safety, our friends (and family) can also affect our emotional well-being. We must take notice of the tendencies and habits of the people in our lives. Are they manipulative, compulsive, selfish, and mean spirited? Even if they do not exhibit these qualities with us right now, do they exhibit these qualities with others? Are our friends and family members docile, un-opinionated, and living afraid? Why? Are they constantly telling us what we should be doing and how we should be living? If we choose not to follow their advice, how do they respond- are they accepting, or disrespectful, rude, and condescending? Do they talk about ideas and concepts, or do they gossip about people and discuss reality TV exclusively? Are they happy for us when great things happen, or are they actually jealous? These things really matter.

Sometimes it is necessary to set boundaries with certain people. Setting boundaries is nothing to be afraid of, and it is not always a contact sport. Some people do not even realize they are sitting outside a boundary that I erected due to how their behavior and habits impacted me. If a boundary is required, there is usually no need to announce it. Just do it. We should all be serious about the company we keep.

Do Away with Fear

Another factor that can impact how you live is fear. What is going to happen if I change this habit that I have leaned on for the last twenty years? How will this person react if I don't answer their daily phone call and listen to them complain for two hours and let them cut me off whenever I try to talk about me. What if I stop allowing this other person to speak to me any kind of way? I am afraid to change and challenge the status quo. What might happen?

I used to be afraid to challenge people and set boundaries. I was once afraid to change what I was doing. When I acknowledged that I was afraid to change, afraid of doing things differently, afraid to confront, I was actually acknowledging that fear was controlling me, and that was hard to admit. Bearing in mind that God did not give us the spirit of fear, and in order to live better than I was living, I had to take a chance, despite the fear. Sometimes the best thing to do is to take the chance despite the fear. The result might be your best life.

Finding My Purpose

What is my purpose? Why am I here? I used to think that there was one answer to that question for every person. For example, a teacher's purpose is to share knowledge and inspire, a police officer's purpose is to protect and serve. A doctor's purpose is to diagnose and treat. But as I have matured, I have come to realize that purpose is much more complex than that. And I also believe that one's purpose shifts and changes with time, and your purpose can be different with each person you encounter.

Now, I believe that Purpose is your assignment from and obedience to God. When I was chronologically young (and also a baby Christian), my assignments were simple compared to the assignments that He has given to me over the years as I have matured. Once my assignments were things like spend time with your nieces, offer a listening ear to your step-child. However, as I matured the nature of His assignments changed. For example, when I was debating whether to attend a gathering in memory of my former husband, I asked God what I should do. He told me to "do the right thing". The Lord did not provide any specifics about "the right thing", but I knew what the right thing was and I knew I could not pretend that I did not know. I showed up at the gathering even though initially, I was reluctant to do it. It turns out that I benefitted from being there, but more than that, my attendance was welcomed and much needed by certain family members. Thus I fulfilled a purpose in that particular season. On that day, my purpose had absolutely nothing to do with my gifts and abilities. It had everything to do with humanity. I completed an assignment in obedience to Him and in doing so, served as a conduit bringing a measure of His comfort to His people.

Generally, we tend to limit the definition of purpose. We put purpose in a box and incorrectly define purpose by connecting it to what we do as a job or profession or according to the gifts, skills, and abilities that we possess.

In fact, our purpose is revealed when we listen to and obey God in service to his people.

Walking in Vision

When I began to consider what I actually believe about vision, my thoughts took an unexpected turn to a highly regarded children's book and snippets of memories about conversations overheard during childhood.

The children's book, <u>The People Who Could Fly</u>, is a collection of folk stories about black people. The book was written in the 1980s by author Virginia Hamilton. One of the stories in the collection concerns a group of enslaved black people who remembered they could fly, and when this fact came to their remembrance, they flew away from the awful circumstances they were experiencing. The folk tale in Ms. Hamilton's book is related to the stories told about a group of slaves on the Georgia coast. These stories resonated with snippets of memories of conversations that I overheard as a child.

When I was little, I would listen to the adults in my family when they talked about their childhoods, and when they told stories of our elders and ancestors. I recall pieces of all sorts of stories that seemed incredible and fanciful at the time. One piece of a memory that I possess concerns people who could fly. I do not recall details or where I heard the story or which elder shared the information, but I remember hearing about Black people who could fly.

What do stories about people who could fly have to do with vision? Everything. It was not necessary for the people who could fly to call upon anything that they did not already possess in order to ascend. Nobody came (or was coming) to save them. Instead, they had to reach within and call up their knowledge and realization of their own abilities. They did the internal work that made it possible for them to realize they could fly, and with that realization, they took to the sky. We too can take flight if we do the work of looking inside so that we can remember/realize everything we are capable of.

Vision requires introspection and action. We make the vision boards and write beautiful vision statements for ourselves and our businesses. That is not and never has been enough.

What steps do we take to make the vision real? Do we ask ourselves the difficult questions and dig out and use the knowledge and abilities that lie within us? Do we boldly go forward with the commitment and confidence that are required if we are planning to actually take to the sky?

We have been blessed with all sorts of gifts and abilities that are wonderful and magical. Sadly, too often we allow the magic (the vision) to lie dormant, and once dormant, the magic/the vision is eventually forgotten.

I am hopeful that we will all do the work required to make the magic/the vision live. We must look within, identify our knowledge and abilities, and act on them with confidence and commitment. All of us can fly.

Closing Remarks on Life, Vision, and Purpose

As we continue the path of life, we will also continue to encounter turns, twists, ups, downs, wins and losses. And even though we might not understand some of the things we encounter, be assured that everything is part of the process. That is the process of who you are continually evolving into each and every day. No experience will be found unuseful. Take notes and make lots of memories. Pursue your vision at every costs! It will speak for you! Your vision will tell the story of who you are, where you see yourself going, what you see yourself doing, and who you see yourself become. Your vision is a reflection of who you are, from the inside out. Lastly, discover and embrace your purpose. It gives your life meaning, and answers the question of why you exist!

Now go and make your contribution to the world!!!